Attributes
of an
Aquarius

Ashly E. Smith

Illustrator/Concept Developer:
Ashly E. Smith

Graphic Artist:
Jansina with Rivershore Books

ISBN 978-0-692-24670-2

Dedication

To all of my muses

Table of Contents

Introduction

Who is she? Many times, she is delightful. She is friendly to those who do not deserve it, and honest even when she doesn't want to be. She is loyal to those closest to her, although at times she does not receive it in return. She is inventive, and independent, even when she needs someone. Because of her emotional trials, she can become intractable. At times, contrary and unpredictable. Other times detached. Why? Ask her no questions, and she will tell you no lies. C'est la vie. Take a journey with her as she adjusts to life through her eyes, while balancing herself upon her stepping-stones. What are these stepping stones? Impediments? Maybe to you. But to her, these are simply...Attributes of an Aquarius.

The Water Bearer: One who gives life, both symbolically and eternally. One who smiles through strife. One who lifts others up, while feeling down herself. As an Aquarius I'm growth oriented, while being concerned with equality and individual freedom. In the mind of we Aquarians, the water from the vessel seems tainted at times, but it eventually washes away the past pain, leaving room for a fresh new start.

The Water Bearer

Born in February, bitterly cold
No sunshine
Despite this blizzard,
She remained sublime

Through many rights and wrongs
Home stood strong
Despite bleak surroundings
She knew what to choose
Living in the midst of it
She refused
To sing the inner city blues

The Catholic school system
Nurtured her scholastic growth
Lacking the love and attention
That she needed the most

Constantly hid her feelings
Afraid to speak her mind
Fearing the negative opinions
Of those deceitful and unkind

When verbally attacked
She masked her pain
Appearing bone dry
In the pouring rain

Her signature smile
Shows nothing but happiness

In her world
Her dignified confidence
Is as rare as an ancient pearl

Many have tried to shackle her spirit
And shatter her self esteem
Forcing her to realize
That no matter how nice she was
Others could still be mean

Small things bothered her
For the longest time
Causing massive difficulty to unwind

Her family taunted her
Constantly testing her patience
And strength
So called friends were often envious
Of her gifts

While some looked for happiness
Through the accumulation of wealth,
This poised Aquarius
Has always depended on herself

For those who have lost the way
She tries to be their guide
She tackles her own issues
While taking others' in stride

She is destined for greatness
Although it seems
Certain situations and people
Try to devour her cream

Today, she sheds her thoughts
Articulate and free
Allowing nothing or no one
To abolish her glee

She's still drying her tears
Combating her fears
Increasing her strength
Making her wise beyond her years

She has washed away the dirt of worry
And cleaned the scars of doubt
Always knowing that God
Is her only way out

Out of misery
Free of sadness
Clear of the darkness within
Away from negativity
Of those of and closest to kin

With the guidance of the good Lord
By her side
She is a tranquil image
Of serenity filled with
Intelligence and pride

Accepting hearts of gold
Denouncing those of stone
She is the Water bearer
Care for her, love her
Or leave her alone!

It is of vast importance that we love ourselves, but just because we are comfortable in our own skin does not imply that we like being insulted. Many find this hard to believe, but tolerating something and liking it, are two different things. Lovingly sharing jokes has always been acceptable at times, but they have boundaries. Damaging a person's soul because you have a problem with how they present themselves is never a good thing. You don't have to put others down to raise yourself up.

If someone's disposition threatens you that much, excommunicate yourself from them. Even a person with the thickest skin is weakened under attack. It may not seem visible, but it is definitely there. It may feel good for you to obtain laughs at the expense of someone else, but it won't prevail. So remember, the next time you consider defaming someone for personal gain, think of how you would feel if it was done to you

Bruised Not Broken

Yes it's me
The one who was made fun of occasionally
The one who endured the blasphemy
While ignoring them respectfully

Always aimed to please
But often punished for that deed
Always kept a positive mind
In the presence of those who were unkind

My smile offended many
Made them cringe inside
They hoped with all of their might
To weaken my stride

The one who kept big dreams
Despite my family's greed
Never offering offering moral support
For my plans to succeed

The one with boisterous presence
Without being loud
The one who was painfully shy
But stood out amongst the crowd

Sure they tried disrespecting me
Sometimes I allowed them to do so
Wanting friends so badly
I accepted these Oscar winning foes

I couldn't tell the difference then
But I surely can now
As quickly as I welcomed them in
I gladly pushed them out

I see more sunshine now
Rainbows constantly appear
Out of the darkest shadows
Of when fear is near

I dance in the rain
Getting soaked with delight
Washing away all doubt
When the towel was in flight

Thank you Lord for the place that I'm in
An replacing my frown with a constant grin

Yes it's me
Just a mere fraction
But better version of what I used to be

What is a champion? To most sports fans, a champion is a person who has defeated all opponents in a competition. In other words, someone who hold first place. In actuality, a champion is a person who fights for or defends any person or cause.

Defending others is a way of showing that you have a good heart, but what about defending yourself for a change? Before you defend the honor of any other person, place, or thing, you must first defend your own. If you wreck your own self esteem, you make it alright for others to do the same.

Being a champion isn't easy, but nothing worthwhile is. Some days you will feel defeated, but you can't allow that to stop you. Regardless of any stressful situation, as a champion, you must keep your composure. Also keep in mind that being brash doesn't always get you respect. When you behave like a nimrod, more than likely, you will be treated like one.

We have all been criticized by others for being ourselves. We aren't perfect but we have to be us. If we don't want to be doormats, we can't remain on the floor. Getting up is what being a true champion is all about.

Champion

I'm the volcano ready to explode

I know I'm expressive I don't need to be told

Who are you to tell me

That I don't have what it takes

To make the knees of the entire world shake

I've seen the mountain, I'm approaching the top

Until I reach my destination, I won't stop

Never will I leave, I was meant to be here

Taking no prisoners, God is who I fear

If you hate me, I still love you to a small degree

But if you dish no respect, you get none from me

Many places I'm going

I remember where I've been

Never forgot where I came from

I know where Iam

Some tell me I could, I few tell me I should

Tell me I can't, I wish you would

Stand back!

I demand that you let me through

If you refuse to move

I'll be forced to step over you

I'm destined to prosper

Never to succumb

I'm a champion

Look out world

Here I come!

Many people would say that they are content with who they are, therefore they refuse to change. But understand that in order to improve our self knowledge, self awareness, and enhance our lifestyles we must progress to become our better selves. As long as we are changing for the greater good, we can't go wrong.

Metamorphosis

The girl that was once naive
Is now wise
She has shed her pessimism
And her lonely cries

Once overtaken my heartache
She has cried rivers of tears
She has chosen days of hope
Instead of hours spent in fear

This girl's one wish
Is true happiness
An ambition that sometimes
Leads to complete emptiness

This girl once dreamed
Of finding a love of her own
And often encountered
Hearts carved in stone

This girl is much stronger
Than before
She has the motivation
And drive to become more

This girl has grown
Into an exotic flower
A beauty given to her
By God's highest power

This girl will continue to be
The best she can be
Who is this girl?
She is me

What do many models and celebrities have in common? They all have an undeniable beauty that attracts us to them. Even we regular people have a self esteem boost when we look better. Clothes, hair, shoes, makeup, and jewelry all sound wonderful. So what's the catch?

These things all are admired then duplicated and eventually discarded. Translation: Looks fade, even if you try to keep them fresh and new. Physical beauty can be a tricky thing, because it's the first thing that you see. Attractive people are very easy on the eyes. Once distracted by the pretty eyes and nice smiles on these people, we must meet them.

Some will flatter us, some won't. There is nothing more disappointing than a desirable person not behaving the way that they look. What does this mean? A beautiful heart is more appealing and lasts much longer than any other physical assets or material things. Its never becomes dated. Stop allowing misfortunes to force you to realize this. It's never too late.

The Meaning of Beauty

What is Beauty?

Some say, a girl that's a cutie

Huh! Maybe in a movie!

True beauty comes from within

It is not inherited from our kin

Or created with a pencil or pen

Once beauty is found within ourselves

We don't need anything from anyone else

A beautiful person is someone who is kind

One with a caring heart and mind

Possessing true beauty

Will make your dreams come true

Just remember that it starts inside of you

Loving yourself is where beauty begins

You'll never feel like a loser You'll always win

Beauty is confidence, beauty is grace

Always possess it, anytime anyplace

Beautiful people,

you know the deal

Believe in yourself

Or no one else will

A positive Spirit is rare, which is why although they may get bruised, we can not allow them to be broken. Those who constantly try to dismantle a person's spirit only do so because they have none. Always let the beauty of your spirit shine though. No one can take it away unless you freely give it to them.

Spirit

It's ever present in my smile

And constantly revealed in my style

It has become my identity

And will follow me through infinity

Keeps me grounded while facing pain

Remains my shelter from the menacing rain

It allows me to strive and pursue

While believing in myself

When others refuse

See it, feel it, hear it, My spirit

My grandmother, Doray Johnson, was one of the strongest women that I knew. Working full time and raising 5 kids practically on your own is something that many women can't say that they've done. Imagine living your life day to day, handling your responsibilities, only to find out that you've developed an ailment that threatens your life. This is something that many (males and females alike) wouldn't handle well. When God welcomed her through his heavenly gates, I was 9 years old and just beginning life. Still to this day I remember certain lessons that she taught me.

Once I reached adulthood and started navigating through the book of life, I longed for her guidance, as she never judged me. But like many angels, God only shares them with us for a short time. She had done all that she could do on Earth, and it was time for her to rest. Although I miss her, I know that she's eternally happy now.

Grandmother's Soul

A woman so distinguished and wise

With undying love in her eyes

She was carved lovely and smart

Resembling a piece of art

Her hugs were as gentle as silk

And more nurturing than milk

She remained determined and hardworking

Despite the danger lurking

Concern and grace

Were constantly present on her face

Despite experiencing turmoil through the years

She never revealed her tears

As steady as the rain

Stress often flooded her brain

She had given each day her best

Now it was time to rest

As peaceful as a bird that sings

Heaven blessed this angel with wings

Floating as freely as a butterfly

She gladly kissed her problems goodbye

Young or old, no piece of gold

Shines as bright

As my grandmother's soul

When God creates an angel, he fills it with the most majestic splendor and grace. He then sends that angel to Earth to share its light and love. While the angel is working God watches closely. When he feels that the angel has served it purpose, he takes it back. That is why Micheal Jackson is resting now. He was created with a miraculous talent and spirit that made us smile and cry at the same time. When I was a little girl, I can recall the first time that I saw him on television. The way he moved, his voice, and how great his music sounded, was amazingly enthralling. He was unlike anyone, I had ever seen.

"Mommy look!" Michael is on!" I would beam with glee. To me, he was so magical, almost like a musical superhero. He made me so happy and excited, regardless of what mood that I was in. He made my childhood, like many others, so wonderful and sweet. The irony is that he compromised his own childhood in the process. The entire time that he was on stage and in music videos pleasing us, he was hiding his own pain. I don't know many people who can smile through the pressures of the entire world being on their shoulders. Although some time has passed since he left, I still speak of him in the present tense. Why? Because it's hard to lose someone of his caliber. The world is short of people who have the same heart as he possessed. Neither his music nor his spirit will ever become extinct.

Rest in eternal peace MJ.

Innovator

August 29, 1958 marked the birth
Of one of God's most precious works

With moves that put you in a trance
He gives a whole new meaning to the word dance

He's enigmatic. A mystical dream.
One of the most amazing performers the world has ever seen

He is a musical sensation
The burns the soul like ultraviolet radiation

His eyes sparkle with curiosity
Hiding distant animosity

He has a smile that lights up any room
Accompanied by a spirit which reflects the joy of a sunny after-
noon

He is a comfort zone to those who feel alone
With the power to melt any heart made of stone

Often criticized for his controversial beliefs
He is constantly the target of unethical creeps

He faces obstacles with a child's heart
Allowing heartache to vanish before it starts

Audiences touched by this genius are both excited and frantic
For he possesses a voice that is both aggressive and romantic

This miraculous spirit has a heart of gold
Enhanced by a brilliant mind and beautiful soul

A magnetic force that leaves audiences with awe and satisfaction
He is the dynamic, incomparable Michael Jackson

When two are in love, or even in like with one another, the feeling of closeness is essential. Holding hands, caressing faces, stroking the hair, and staring into the eyes, are only mere examples of the affections shown. At times hugging, and shaking hands isn't enough. We must be entrapped in this person's embrace, never wanting to be released. This poem was actually inspired by all the times that I have been held when I needed it the most.

Holding Me

Your arms are my shelter from the rain
Shielding my heart from any piercing pain

When my love is in flight
Capture me, entrap me
Squeeze me tight

If all around us vanishes, one could still see
The pristine tranquil image of you
Holding me

The mind enables consciousness, perception, thinking, judgment and memory. The main question regarding the nature of the mind is its relation to the physical brain and nervous system. Many philosophers seem to have it figured out, but as humans, we have many things that trigger certain emotions: Our values, morals, and what we've experienced as a whole. At times we experience confusion, such as, sadness during happy times. I know I have. Always remember that no matter how complex things get, the power of prayer helps to sort it all out.

Mind of Mine

Seen as a social butterfly
Yet I like being alone
Eager to text,
But ignoring the phone

I like giving affection,
Hardly receiving it return
I'm always thinking
Yet I have lots to learn

Keeping friends and enemies close
Is an art
Although sometimes
I find it difficult
To tell them apart

I love to laugh,
But don't find many things funny
Tired of working like a slave
But I like making money

Music is my escapism
Keeping me sane
During trying times
My brain is overflows
Yet I have peace of mind

When I speak out loud
At times I hear silence
Is everyone playing pretend?

It isn't their lack of listening
They just can't comprehend

Why do I bother
Caring about some things?
And transforming simple minds?
Because I have a big heart that smiles
Even when it wants to cry

Life is a constant struggle
But things will be alright
Through any amount of darkness
I can always see the light

At times I feel isolated,
But I'm surrounded
By unconditional love
From my father and friend,
The good Lord above

"When you have a pack of haters, you're doing something right." This is one of the most overrated statements used. We use this to comfort ourselves at times when really we're annoyed at the mere thought of someone disliking or degrading us for simply being ourselves. We want others to notice our achievements and praise us for them, not purposely try to bring us down. There is no to need to speak negatively about someone because they're trying to do better, and you aren't.

If someone already has something that you want maybe it's their time to have it. They have their time, and you will eventually have yours. Patience is a virtue, even if you're a person of action and not wishful thinking. It's senseless to waste energy bashing someone else when you can put that same energy in to propelling yourself to greatness. Wasted energy is the same as wasted time. Once it's gone you can't get it back.

Ode to the Haters

Leave me alone nimrods!
I'm tired of your very existence
Vanish you idiots!
Damn your extreme persistence

Must you bother me because
I'm more appealing than you?
Or because I don't have a nasty
Disposition like you do?

I'm a winner! A positive force!
If you have complaints
The problem is yours

Despite what you say
I don't have my nose in the air
So to hell with you
And your piercing stares

What have I done to you?
Besides be myself?
My traits are by nature
Not for my health

Stay away from me peons!
I don't wish to have you near
If you say something rude about me
I can always hear

Take your negativity
And shove it up your a**
I don't have time for your stupidity
I have class

Don't you dare try to damage my soul
Continue to play games with your own

Positive people are your worse enemy
Successful people are your biggest fear
If it were up to me
I would make all of you worthless haters
disappear!

Attitude builds character. Does it matter if it's good or bad? Of course it does. Many of us seem to think that if we're brash or abrasive that it will force people to respect us. The reason that many of us believe that this is true, is because we see others become successful as a result of it.

Don't be fooled. What works for others, may not work for you. You have to you use your own mind. Following behind someone else who got away with something negative, does not prove that you will have the same outcome. You must also realize that these same people who you imitate won't be held responsible for your actions.

If you think that being pleasant is overrated, you seriously need to reevaluate. Wearing the word foul as a badge of honor, means that your luck will eventually run out. Evil never prevails. One who purposely disrespects someone, usually does so under the impression that they will be forgiven. Sure forgiveness is the Godly way, but realistically you reap what you sow. If you think that a Black heart feels no pain, think again.

Black Heart

With the blackest of hearts I don't know pain
To many that is most insane

Enemies fear me
Friends have doubts
With the blackness inside, all I can do without

Immortal I seem
I don't worry at all
I don't need anyone to cushion my fall

But who says I will?
I don't cry
Slate legend as my moniker when I die

Do you think that I'm lying? Do you know the truth?
If your answer is yes, your name is fool

No one can hurt me
I can get away with everything no matter who's around
I float on the clouds
I never touch the ground

Reality Check
Who am I?
What have I become?
How could I not change before my time on Earth was done?

I really blew it
Its no ones fault but my own

Because I chose to possess a heart carved in stone

I apologize for not caring enough
To smile and not to frown
For being too selfish to spread love around

Everyone be sure to cherish your time here
For we all are uncertain as to when the end is near

Love your enemies
Keep your friends close
Follow the right path even when others disclose

Realize your dreams, keep God first
Know that only HE can shield you from the worst

In stressful situations, keep your cool
Patience starts inside of you

In the shadow of doubt, keep hope alive
Remember that no one with a black heart survives

It is often easy to blame others for our shortcomings. Although at times the outcome of a situation could be the other person's fault, we must also see the role that you played as well, and to accept responsibility for the result. This tactic is often mastered through lots of critical thinking and soul searching. This is also a time to prove how your level of maturity surpasses those who hurt you.

The Blame Game

I blame you for all that's wrong

You're the reason

For these bitter lyrics

In my song

If you had been different

Perhaps all would be well

Absent would be this animosity

That I continuously dwell

You've been there for others

But not me

You're totally blind

 To what you think you see

I looked to you for happiness

Assuming that you could deliver

Unwisely handing you my canvas

To paint the perfect picture

Navigating through life,

We can't help who we meet

Why did I get close to you?

I guess that part is on me

During my reflection periods, I often dream of reaching nirvana. I usually view my life as it was, and how it is currently, constantly wondering if such a thing is possible. At times my reflections bring bits of pessimism and self doubt. Many of these feelings were results of others not believing in me. Family, so-called friends, even complete strangers.

If someone else chooses to shun you, it's their prerogative. This only happens because these individuals are insecure about themselves, and are making an attempt to lift their own spirits by combating yours. Sadly, this type of behavior is a never ending saga. Although I'm still realizing this, I have a better understanding now than when I was younger. "One Day" is my promise to myself that my dreams will soon be realized. Yours will be also. All it takes is a little faith. Anyone who doubts this can think whatever they like. Stay focused.

One Day

One day I'll have whatever I want
Many a fancies and fantasies to flaunt

Mountains of money to carelessly spend
My abundance of cash flow will never end

Gone will be the days of countless bills
Sitting unpaid and unfulfilled

Forfeiting my days of finding treasure
Ruining chances to indulge in my guilty pleasures

I'm ready to travel the world
Visit the places which I've never seen

Away from littered sidewalks
Into the clean and pristine

I need new clothes and shoes
Upon each paycheck I always have to choose

What's the point of working, if I'm always broke?
The mere thought of this always makes me choke

Words can't explain how tired of this I am
This is so deranged!!!

I'm not complaining anymore
Its time for a change

It's going to be a challenge
A game I must play

This feeling of dismay
It ends today

I'll keep my faith in God and my soul intact
Allowing nothing or no one to throw me off track

Optimistic I am
Pessimistic I'm not
All of my pain will eventually rot

Away from my heart
Away from my brain
Away from the harshness of the rain

The clouds will clear
The sunshine will appear
Looking forward to many abundant years

I'm gonna keep on going
Until it's my time to play

Yes, things will change for the better…..One day

Manual labor is something that we all must do to survive. Some of us are blessed to have occupations that we enjoy; however many of us are forced into jobs that we don't like just to obtain a dollar. Many say that money is the root of all evil. At times it can be. But we must be honest with ourselves.

Without money we forfeit our chances for survival and living our lives in the way that we choose. Sure it's important to indulge in your passion, but what's the point in working when you can't enjoy the fruits of your labor? You can't function properly without fuel in your tank, due to having an empty refrigerator. Believe me, I've been there, and its no fun at all. Without straying too far away from my point, I'll say that no matter how much we love or dislike our jobs, it's always good to breathe a sigh of relief, when it's all over for the day, or evening.

Final Hour

My work is done
My freedom has officially come

I'm going home to be alone
Far from people with hearts of stone

My tasks is over for today
Everything is now okay

I have grown tired from working hard
Some peoples' idiotic personalities I can now discard

One sweet day my job will bring devout pleasure
A feeling that I will always treasure

But until I reach this divine power
I will always long for that final hour

We all have those moments when it seems as if nothing goes right. This was written during a time when too much was happening all at once. Being at odds with family members, parting ways with associates whom I thought were friends, and of course being seemingly stuck in dead end jobs. There could have been another river named for the amount of tears that I shed during this time. Although painful ordeals that we face can sometimes threaten to cripple us, we must not allow them to.

Obstacles are tests of both faith and strength, and we have to believe that we will get through them. Remember, God never gives us more than we than handle. Don't ever allow negativity to defeat you. In the end, it simply isn't worth it.

Consumed

I often feel consumed by the obstacles around me
They are the darkest shadows of my misery

Inside my eyes are drops of rain
Forcefully released by clouds of pain

I pray to God for his supernatural strength
That can allow these piercing showers to end

Reflection periods are sometimes riddled with disbelief
And flooded with agonizing grief

I sometimes ask myself why
Are shades of gray in blue skies?

Please help me Lord to know
That my wilted flowers can continue to grow

Lead me to that miraculous meadow
The path to my special rainbow

At the end of the rainbow is my pot of gold
For I am consumed nevermore

To me, blue is the color of pain. It comes in many immaculate shades, which is why we become attracted to it, but it still reflects sadness. Brainstorm on this theory as much as you wish, just don't let the title fool you. Although I am speaking of a human, and not an object or color, I'm not referring to a male. While writing, "Mr." just seemed to fit. To me, it speaks of someone who is a negative factor, both physically and emotionally.

Of course this could be a male or female. During my time on Earth, I'm come across quite a few Blues. They no longer exist in my life and never will again. Having a Blue around, not only weakens your heart, but your spirit as well. The only person that should have that type of control over you, if you allow it, is yourself

Mr. Blue

I stand alone, dodging numerous stones
Being viciously thrown

As the clouds roll in, I see someone
A figure who despises fun

A spirit who brings the rain
And has a zest for pain

Who he is, I haven't the slightest clue
So I'll slate him Mr. Blue

Blue, Who are you?
How did you find me?

I believe that I've seen you before
The night when you closed the door

On my hopes and dreams
And ripped my heart at the seams

The day that brown leaves replaced the green
And individuals once kind turned against me

Why have you cast this upon me?
I don't care to be bothered by you, you see?

You always belittle me for trying
You roar with laughter, at the sight of me crying

Vanish!!!!! Disappear!!!!
I do not wish to have you near

I've seen many things, met all kinds
Some continue to change, right before my eyes

I've kept the old, welcomed the new
But have never encountered one as cruel as you
Mr. Blue

A first friend, a first kiss, a first love, a first car, a first house, a first job, a child's first steps. Many firsts are irreplaceable. One of life's greatest disappointments is when we try to recreate these firsts and it doesn't happen. Even if the firsts are not as grand, the symbolic thing is that, as your life improves, you can reflect upon them and think, Wow!!! I have really come a long way. In contrast, at times the firsts are exceptional, proposing the question, "Why are things never as good as they are the first time around? Very perplexing I know.

The First

Everyday people
The sight
The smile
Simplistic style

Upon each greeting
Many mirror shyness
During chance meetings

Almost immediately
The sun's transparent rays are suddenly gleaming

Drifting to another time and place
After the priceless glimpse of each face

Getting to know one's soul well
Digesting secrets only close confidants can tell

Individuals change day after day
Revealing any baggage the heart can convey

Friends come, Friends go
Life expectancy? No one knows

On many occasions, one has wondered
With extreme thirst, and devout hunger

How different situations can arise?
Ignoring each lost soul's lonely cries?

How certain things can be extremely grand?
With leery refusal to expand?

These questions remain unanswered
Causing one to convert

To conversations with God
To seize the confusion and hurt

This is the road that I have taken
Hoping that from each negative nightmare
All can be awakened

Creative thinkers reluctantly succumb
To convulsions with matters of the heart
Stopping all positivity before it starts

Many social individuals, to whom cruelty suddenly shown
Eventually become hermits
Choosing to be alone

Trickery of the mind, can almost seem as a curse
To still not know the reason

Why nothing ever remains as good as the first

We have many theories about the rain. Some think it reflects sadness. Some think it ruins fun outings. Many have their own opinion, but to me, rainfall is simply God's tears. He sheds them to cleanse the Earth, washing away its pain and strife.

In other words, the rain produces tranquility. So what happens when thunder comes? Although thunder is loud, forceful, and frightening, it is simply God speaking to us. What he is saying we may not fathom, but his tone always forces us to listen. I've always been taught never to move during a storm.

"Sit still, while God does his work" my mother would say. I didn't understand then, but I do now. I wrote this one during a rainy Friday afternoon. It only features a minor rhyme scheme, not a full one. I was staring out my window, and wanted to capture the true amazement of how God's work can really move people.

Thunder Claps

Calm afternoon
Sitting, staring outside my window
I admire how brightly the sun is shining
The birds are happily frolicking through the sky

People constantly moving
Some with places to go
Some without a care in the world

Suddenly the sun disappears
The clouds roll in
The rain starts pouring down

Everyone scurries in fear

Thunder claps
I hope there's no lightening
The thunder alone, is already frightening

The rain
How it delicately washes my windows
Looks beautiful from the inside

What if I was outside with everyone else?
Getting wet and hurriedly running for shelter?

Of course I would survive. I would have no choice
There would be no point in being afraid

The rain is so heavy against my window

It's hard for me to see what's going on now

Thunderclaps
I hope there's no lightening
The thunder alone is already frightening

The sound seems lighter now
My windows are still a bit blurry
But I think the rain has stopped

Yes it did! Look at the sky!
The clouds have disappeared
The sun seems to be peeking through

The birds have returned
The people are back also
It's like they never left

Indeed the thunderclaps have ceased

I'm glad that there was no lightening
The thunder alone was already frightening

Mysterious, brilliant, and androgynous are just a mere three words to describe Prince. He has enchanted many for years, and is one of the most prolific entertainers in the universe. With a spirit as regal as his name, he presents a version of the human form that no one has ever seen before. With flamboyant flair, he commands each stage with impeccable prowess, and over the years he's transformed into a better version of his already phenomenal being. I've always admired how he could separate both worlds.

His electrifying stage presence, and his reserved natural demeanor makes him even more intriguing. In addition to relishing his music, I also still watch Purple Rain and Under the Cherry Moon with vast enjoyment. I must also add that seeing him perform on television is nothing compared to seeing him live. I've been lucky enough to do so twice. Keep shining Mr. Nelson. You do it so well.

The Best

June 7, 1958 presented God's idea from afar
Upon your creation, he knew that you were a star.

You are blessed with enthralling musical ability
Accompanied with a brilliant mind
In today's music that is extremely hard to find

You spread your love from East to West
Which is why I consider you the best

Many have challenged
Your puzzling theories
You gracefully handled all adversity

Continue to be you unique I think that you should
Because to be great is to be misunderstood

You have brought your purple passion
To every land

You can hypnotize any audience
With one wave of your hand

Your voice showcases impeccable versatility
With bass and falsettos
That are equally bone chilling

You have mastered all instruments
Like a true virtuoso
Which is the pinnacle

Of your spectacular stage shows

You have a miraculous spirit
That shines through and through
Which is why the world adores you

You're a spectacular being with a divine sense
A rare and regal essence simply known as Prince

Like a bird whose wings will never rest
You are, and will always be, the best

Ahhh.... escapism. A mental, and at times, physical journey away from the daily struggles of life. As you already know, escaping is always a blissful when its experienced alone. But imagine the exstacy of experiencing it with someone special. While reading this poem, allow your minds to wander.

Sweet Escape

The sun
How brightly it shines
Your hand clasped tightly with mine

The peaceful waters
As freely as they flow

Mesh beautifully with the breeze
As gently as it blows

Frolicking about, playfully in the sand
We sail away to our intimate land

Beneath the palm trees
I'll hold you close to my heart

Wishing that we'd never part

No one but us, and the birds who sing
I feel as if I have everything.

Everything I want
Everything I need

Paradise is here
Follow my lead

We all have or have had our crushes. Whether in reality or fantasy, these people have the ability to make any form of darkness disappear. Nothing is ever wrong when they're around, or on the television or movie screen. What is it that draws us to these people? Their smile? Their distinctive charm? Or is it their breathtaking beauty? More than likely the answer is all of the above. It's an unspeakable joy to feel the aura of these people on a personal level, but sometimes it's just as much pleasure to simply imagine.

Cozy

Slowly walking

Sweetly talking

Into my heart he comes

With the warmest smile

The slickest style

I feel the wrath of his love

Where did he come from?

No one knows

I may have seen him before

I'm not sure

He's captivating, he keeps the sunlight dwelling

He's devastating, as well as, compelling

His compliments flatter me

They make my cheeks so rosy

His hugs entrap me, as he tightly grasps me

A feeling that is simply cozy

Being in love is a splendid thing, although it will be met with many challenges. There's nothing like finding and building a life with the one that you love, and having that person love you in return. The feeling in general is rare, yet enthralling. Many believe that it doesn't exist. Others assume that by adoring someone else, they can unknowingly lose themselves in the process.

Honestly, the theories are endless. Conversing with multiple people on the matter will generate multiple answers. Some you will agree with, some you won't. You have to draw your own conclusions. The average person, no matter how long their relationships have lasted, can't define the true meaning of love.

Identical to friendship, love is something that we judge for ourselves. Only you know what you can and can not tolerate. No one can make that decision for you. In the end, our soul mates are ones that we can't live with, or without. Puzzling huh? Not really. When you can look at this person and see reflections of yourself, it is no question that you want to be with this person for the rest of your life.

Close Our Eyes

You're the wave that I ride at its highest tide

The current that transforms darkness to light

The celestial silence that helps me sleep at night

With arms of tenderness holding me tight

A voice as sweet as birds singing in tune

A spirit that shines as bright as the moon

Transfixing me with your come hither stare

Softly touching me

Showing how much you care

That loving gaze deep into my eyes

Paralyzing any thoughts of lonely cries

You tell me that you love me each and everyday

Words that I long to hear you say

You're that friend to the end

That I can forever trust

Something I've always wanted

And needed so much

My life is so beautiful with you here

Words as true, as crystal is clear

We're two of a kind, yet one of the same

Into my world, I'm so glad that you came

With each laugh we share, and each tear we cry

I pray that God will keep us together

Until the day that we forever

Close our eyes

What is marriage? Holy matrimony? The legal joining of two people? Wedded bliss? The answer is all of the above. We all dream of finding our soul mates. The ones to share the spice of life, as well as the lows, taking breaks to hold, console, and eventually grow old with them. The moment when just the sound of this person's voice can excite you, and you always want to be alone with them is the best feeling in the world. Marriage is that sacred bond that shouldn't ever be broken, but it takes both parties to strengthen that bond. To find this is a true blessing so if you don't have it, seek it, once you have it, hold on tightly to it.

To My Future Husband

You are filled with wonderment and delight

At times you blissfully keep me awake at night

Always making me feel that beautiful way

Bringing me much joy throughout the day

You're intriguing

Amazing, and magnificent,

Molded together as one

As radiant as a reflection of the sun

The positivity that you generate

Seems unreal

I'm still in awe of the way

That you make me feel

I'm staying upon this cloud

For as long as I can

Floating freely and happily,

As my enchantment would never end

Never disappear, stay for awhile

For you are the reason

For my constant smiles

My knight with amour that shines so bright

Let's innocently portray two kids at play

As we prepare to walk down the aisle one day

High self esteem is essential in this corrupt world of ours. It must always remain intact, on the account that there are always going to be spirit snatchers around us. My spirit snatchers are the ones that inspired this poem. How do we abolish them? Is it even possible? Sure it is.

Keep your mind on pleasing God, and not human beings who are breathing the same air that you are. Following this advice is extremely challenging, and new tactics will be learned with each passing day. These lessons will often be tested, and the outcomes will often bring much disdain and heartache. These atrocities will occur mostly if the culprits inflicting the pain are ones that we currently or have once cared about. Those of us with love in our hearts will want to spread it around freely; however, we must love ourselves before we can ever dream of loving someone else.

This applies to all relationships and friendships. The best that we can be is ourselves. Others can choose whether or not they want to love us in return.

Cinnamon Sun

A naive little Black girl

Becomes a woman now wise

She has shed her pessimism

And her lonely cries

She is one who is kind

With a loving heart and mind

A pristine fortress

Statuesque and strong

She is not always right

But she is barely wrong

She has grown as gracefully

As flowers in the spring

And has been blessed to break

The barriers of anything

She has confidence, style and grace

She always carries it in good taste

Independence is her badge of honor

Worn with pride

If ever she fails

She takes it in stride

Every gray sky soon vanishes

To make way for the one

Capsule of radiance

Known as the Cinnamon Sun

Conclusion

My attributes have mentally prepared me for all forms of weather. The kind that even the sturdiest raincoat isn't needed for. As a whole, it is only through searching within, that we come to find that we are indeed more resilient than we think we are. We've won, we've lost, we've loved, we've learned, we laughed, and we've cried. Through it all, we are, and will always remain stronger than the person that we were yesterday.

Sometimes she worries
Many times she's proud
Occasionally she weeps
Often she smiles

At times she's had answers
Others she's had to choose
Some would praise her
Others chose to abuse

Often she's challenged
Competing at all costs
Humbled by each win
Learning from each loss

She's been trapped in a box
And covered in doubt
With her strength as her guide
She found her way out

Through all laughter
And all tears cried
She navigates through life
With her head held high

Acknowledgments

First of all I thank God, for realizing my talents when I didn't see them in myself, and giving me the strength to pursue them. Thank you Most High for forgiving my sins and giving me countless opportunities to get things right. My very first novel is a result of your many blessings.

I would also like to thank my mother Elizabeth for introducing me to the world, my little sister Brittany, my stepfather Derek, the rest of my family and my small list of special friends who have also become my extended family(you know who you are).To my relatives in Heaven, I miss you. To BJ, my biggest supporter, and my gift from God, I love you.

To those who have made me smile, or given me a friendly hug, thank you because my heart needs that. I'm also thankful for all of you who have taught me at least one valuable lesson in life. Through any pain that you may have caused, you have indefinitely made me stronger.

On the professional front: Fellow authors Martina Evans, Tyeisha Downer, and Rocky Perry, thank you all for your heartfelt publishing advice. Nadine Comeau, Brandi Jarath, Kira Miles, Brandon Jones, and everyone at the Examiner, thank you all for giving me the chance to showcase my writing skills for your publications. Despite all of the doors that have slammed in my face, you all actually believed in me and for that, I am eternally grateful. To Freepik, the amazing Jansina Grossman and Susan E. Thomas thank you immensely for your contributions in bringing my creation to life.

To all of my faithful supporters on Facebook, Twitter, and my other social networks, thank you abundantly for your friendship. Many of you have become valuable assets to my life and I'm glad that God brought has brought us together. To anyone whose name that I didn't mention, please blame my cluttered head and not my fragile heart. I Love you all.

Rivershore Books

www.rivershorebooks.com
blog.rivershorebooks.com
www.facebook.com/rivershore.books
www.twitter.com/rivershorebooks

Info@rivershorebooks.com

Made in the USA
Charleston, SC
22 February 2015